The Saucy Scoop on Pizza

by Catherine Ipcizade

Consulting Editor: Gail Saunders-Smith, PhD

Consultant: Professor Art Hill
Department of Food Science
University of Guelph

CAPSTONE PRESS
a capstone imprint

Pebble Plus is published by Capstone Press,
151 Good Counsel Drive, P.O. Box 669, Mankato, Minnesota 56002.
www.capstonepub.com

Books published by Capstone Press are manufactured with paper
containing at least 10 percent post-consumer waste.

Library of Congress Cataloging-in-Publication Data
Ipcizade, Catherine.
  The saucy scoop on pizza / by Catherine Ipcizade.
    p. cm.—(Pebble plus. Favorite food facts)
  Includes bibliographical references and index.
  Summary: "Full-color photographs and simple text present fun facts about pizza"—Provided by publisher.
  ISBN 978-1-4296-6662-6 (library binding)
  1. Pizza—Juvenile literature. I. Title. II. Series.
TX770.P58I63 2012
641.8'248—dc22   2011000371

Editorial Credits
Katy Kudela, editor; Heidi Thompson, designer; Svetlana Zhurkin, media researcher; Sarah Schuette, photo stylist;
    Marcy Morin, scheduler; Laura Manthe, production specialist

Photo Credits
Capstone Studio/Karon Dubke, cover, 1, 4–5, 10–11, 13, 19, 20–21, 21 (top right)
Corbis/epa/Jacek Bednarczyk, 15; Gianni Dagli Orti, 7
Getty Images/Dan Herrick, 8–9
Newscom/Getty Images/AFP/Boris Horvat, 16–17

Capstone thanks the staff at Dino's Pizzeria in North Mankato, Minnesota, for their assistance with
    the pizzas in this book.

Note to Parents and Teachers

The Favorite Food Facts series supports national social studies standards related to people,
places, and culture. This book describes and illustrates pizza. The images support early readers
in understanding the text. The repetition of words and phrases helps early readers learn new
words. This book also introduces early readers to subject-specific vocabulary words, which are
defined in the Glossary section. Early readers may need assistance to read some words and to
use the Table of Contents, Glossary, Read More, Internet Sites, and Index sections of the book.

Printed in the United States of America in North Mankato, Minnesota.
032011   006110CGF11

Table of Contents

The Slice on Pizza

Billions of pizzas are made each year! In the United States, 93 percent of people eat pizza at least once a month.

Inventing Pizza

People have put toppings on dough for thousands of years. But the Italians first used the word "pizza" for plain flatbread. By 1889 pizza had toppings.

In 1905 the first pizza shop

opened in New York City.

Lombardi's Pizza was a hit.

People bought slices

for a few cents each.

How It's Made

Spin! Toss! Catch!
To shape pizza dough,
many chefs spin the dough
in the air. Tossing the dough
makes a softer pizza crust.

Sauce tops the dough.

Next come the toppings.

Wait! Don't forget the cheese.

Now the pizza is ready

for a hot oven.

Imagine That!

Chefs in Poland made one of
the world's longest pizzas.
It stretched more than
3,000 feet (900 meters) long.
That's a lot of pizza!

There are many ways to serve a pizza. But have you tried a pizza cone? Served in Europe, these cones are a fast food treat.

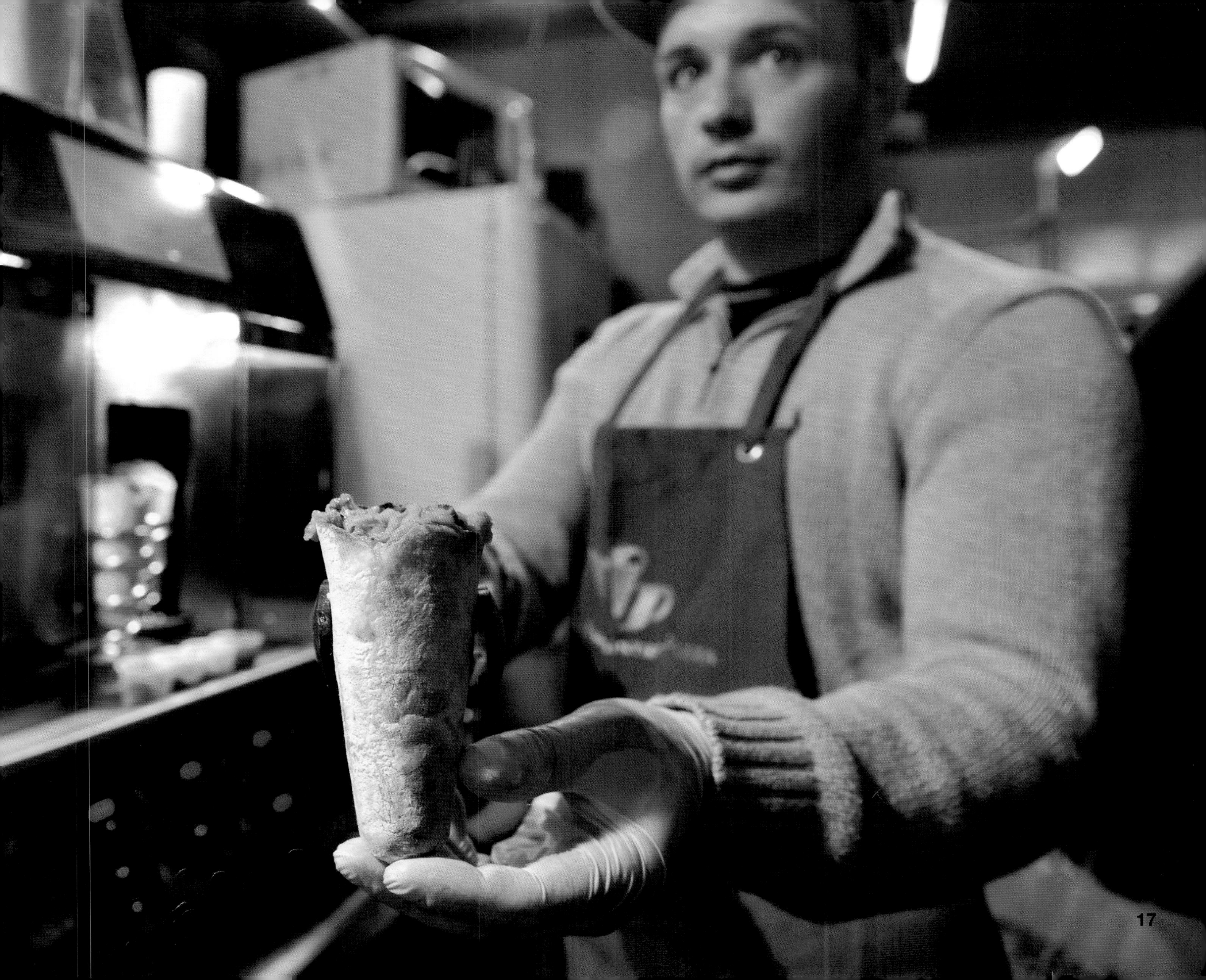

Some pizzas are a sweet treat.

Peanut butter and jelly is

more than a sandwich.

It is a kind of pizza too!

So many kinds of pizza!
Most Americans choose
pepperoni. But in Russia, people
eat pizza topped with sardines.
How do you like your pizza?

Make a Bagel Pizza Snack

Try this recipe, which turns a bagel into mini pizzas. Be sure to ask an adult to bake the pizza bagels for you.

Makes 2 servings

Here's what you need:

Ingredients	Tools
1 sliced bagel	spoon
½ cup (120 mL) pizza sauce	baking sheet
½ cup (120 mL) shredded	oven mitt
mozzarella cheese	spatula
pizza toppings (optional):	2 plates
sliced tomatoes,	
sliced black olives	

Here's what you do:

1. Preheat oven to 425 degrees Fahrenheit (220 degrees Celsius).
2. Use a spoon to spread pizza sauce on each bagel slice.
3. Sprinkle cheese over each bagel slice. Add tomatoes and black olives.
4. Place pizza bagels on baking sheet.
5. Place pizza bagels in preheated oven and toast for about 10 minutes, or until golden brown.
6. Take out of oven and serve on plates.

Glossary

crust—the crisp, outer layer of pizza

dough—a soft, thick mixture of flour, water, and salt; pizza dough is pounded and stretched to make its shape before it is baked

flatbread—a bread made with flour, water, and salt; the bread dough is baked in flat, round loaves

pepperoni—a spicy beef or pork sausage; sliced pepperoni is a popular pizza topping

sardine—a small fish, often sold in cans as food

sauce—a thick liquid that adds flavor to food; pizza sauce is usually made with tomatoes

Read More

Peterson, Cris. *Extra Cheese, Please!: Mozzarella's Journey from Cow to Pizza.* Honesdale, Pa.: Boyds Mills Press, 2004.

Rau, Dana Meachen. *Pizza.* What's Cooking? New York: Marshall Cavendish Benchmark, 2008.

Internet Sites

FactHound offers a safe, fun way to find Internet sites related to this book. All of the sites on FactHound have been researched by our staff.

Here's all you do:

Visit *www.facthound.com*

Type in this code: 9781429666626

Super-cool stuff! Check out projects, games and lots more at **www.capstonekids.com**

Index

Word Count: 212

Grade: 1

Early-Intervention Level: 20